· COLLECTION ·

My Book of Heavenly Ways

About the Artist

Deb Haas Abell lives with her husband and two children in a cozy home with a picket fence, nestled in a small town in Southern Indiana. She hopes this book will put you in touch with heavenly help and healing...and the angel in you!

About the Author

Molly Wigand lives in suburban Kansas City with her husband and three angelic sons. She's grateful to be able to share her inner angel's thoughts and feelings with you.

Heavenly Ways to Handle Stress

Created and Illustrated by
Deb Haas Abell

Written by
Molly Wigand

Text © 1998 by Molly Wigand
Art © 1998 by Deb Haas Abell
Published by One Caring Place
Abbey Press
St. Meinrad, Indiana 47577

All rights reserved.
No part of this book may be used or reproduced in any manner
without written permission of the publisher, except in the case
of brief quotations embodied in critical articles and reviews.

Library of Congress Catalog Number 98-72643

ISBN 0-87029-320-6

Printed in the United States of America

Stress ~ and the Angel in You

Life is filled with stresses that can take away peace of mind. Thankfully, each of us has an inner angel to help us cope.

The nuggets of wisdom in this book are offered to put you in touch with the angel in you, so that you can have less stress and increase peace. Feel free to jot your thoughts and feelings on the write-on activity pages or, if you prefer, keep your reflections privately in your heart.

May this book help you to hear your angel's message of calm assurance: You are not alone. God's strength and peace are with you every moment of every day.

Set Your Angel Free!

FAITH   JOY   HOPE

Sometimes, being human means going through stressful times. But you can reach deep down inside and tap into the heavenly power within you. Your "inner angel" can help return peace to your heart.

HARMONY ♥ CHARITY ♥ GRACE ♥ GOODNESS

Stop, Look, Listen...

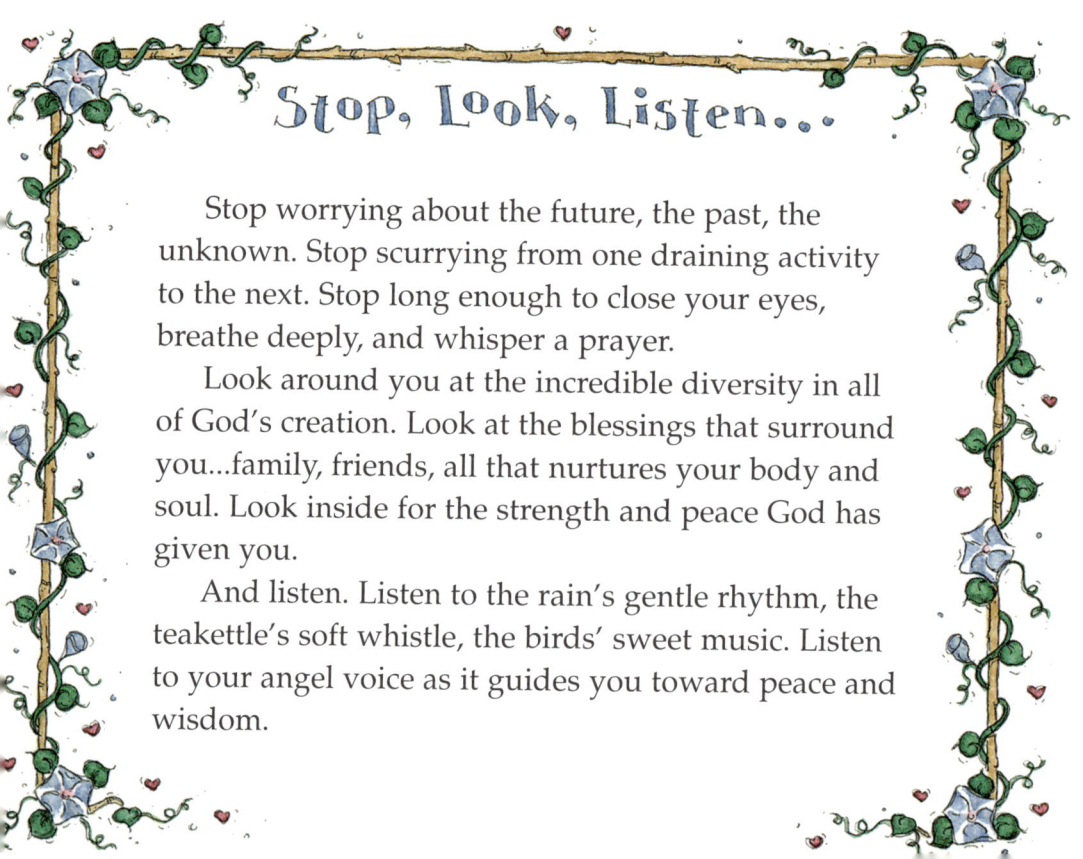

Stop worrying about the future, the past, the unknown. Stop scurrying from one draining activity to the next. Stop long enough to close your eyes, breathe deeply, and whisper a prayer.

Look around you at the incredible diversity in all of God's creation. Look at the blessings that surround you...family, friends, all that nurtures your body and soul. Look inside for the strength and peace God has given you.

And listen. Listen to the rain's gentle rhythm, the teakettle's soft whistle, the birds' sweet music. Listen to your angel voice as it guides you toward peace and wisdom.

♥ Stop for a moment and, in your mind's eye, look back to a more carefree time in your life. What happened to those innocent, joyful days?

♥ Listen for your angel's guidance on how you might recapture today the sense of joy you had back then.

Simply stop, look, and listen.

Keep Your Funny Side Up!

Joy

One sure way to get stress out of your life is to put more joy into it. Have fun! Be funny! Spend time every day with people who make you laugh. Laughter is the music of heaven. A good belly laugh cleanses your soul and relaxes your body. An uncontrollable giggling spree is as good as a cry for releasing pent-up tensions.

Let your angel help you find the humor in every day.

Laugh and your angel laughs with you!

Be a Kid Again!

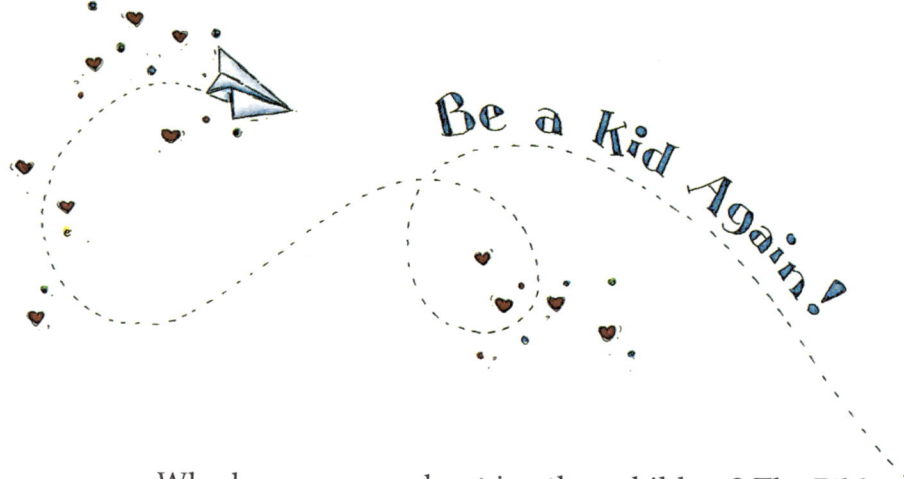

Who knows more about joy than children? The Bible encourages us to be more childlike in our faith and our lives.

Think of young children at play. See them run, laugh, hide, seek, and just enjoy life! Innocence, silliness, and simplicity can help us be happier and more stress-free.

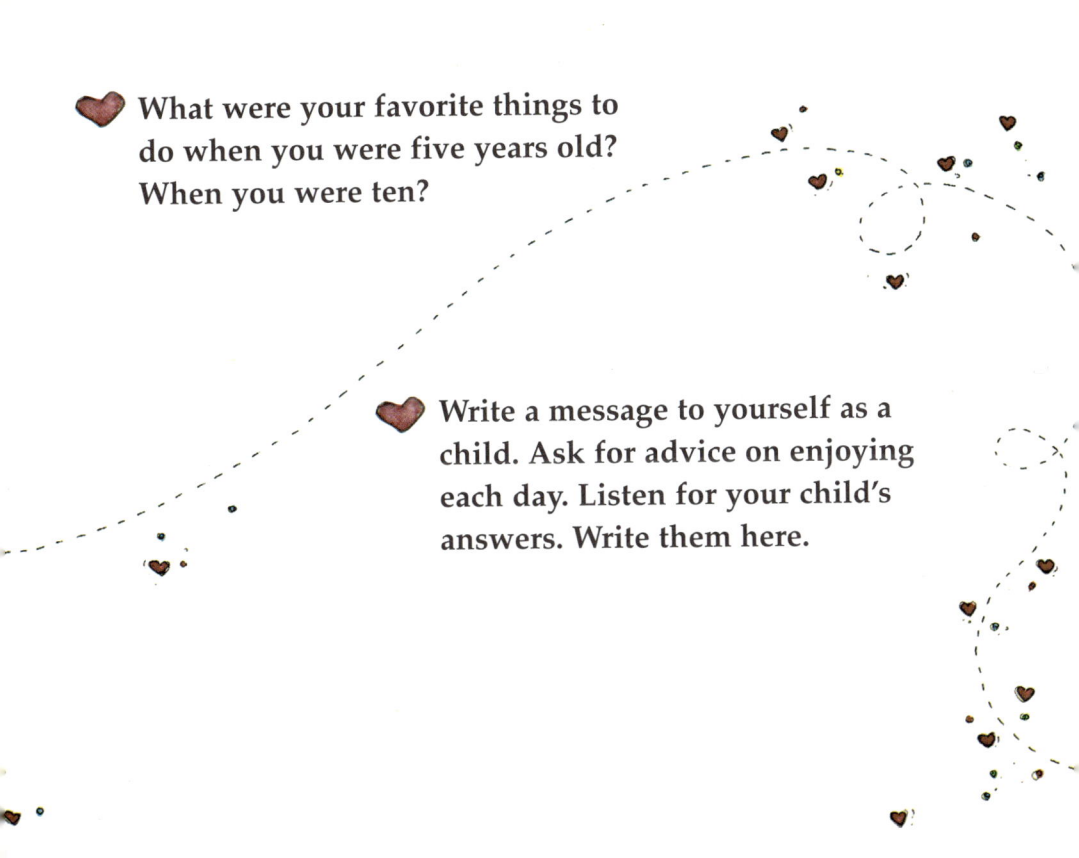

♥ What were your favorite things to do when you were five years old? When you were ten?

♥ Write a message to yourself as a child. Ask for advice on enjoying each day. Listen for your child's answers. Write them here.

Break Away From the ORDINARY

Break free from the "same old, same old." Add some whimsy and fun to your day, and the little aggravations won't seem quite as annoying. Can't find two socks that match in your laundry basket? Wear two different ones. Lots of dust getting you down? Draw a smiley face in it with your finger.

Defy convention. Give yourself rainbow-colored toenails. Face backward in the elevator. Forget your umbrella on purpose.

Break a rule. Do the unexpected. Be just a little bit irresponsible.

Feels great, doesn't it?

God has given each of us the power and desire to create. The angel in you is there to help transform your unique thoughts, feelings, and dreams into creative masterpieces.

Not only sculptors, painters, and poets—but bakers, mothers, and gardeners, too—have creativity and beauty to offer. Any time you add your own personal touch to your daily endeavors, you're practicing your art.

Allow yourself the time and space you need to make your own special magic. It's good for you and those around you when your creative projects take wing.

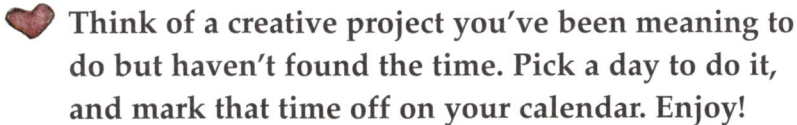

Ignite Your Creative Spark!

Think of a creative project you've been meaning to do but haven't found the time. Pick a day to do it, and mark that time off on your calendar. Enjoy!

Dear God, Thank You for You.

Grace

Practicing gratitude for every big and little blessing keeps our hearts light and our days stress-free.

When you stop to count your blessings, don't forget that faith itself is one of God's most precious gifts. How fortunate we are to have a loving God who provides sustenance not only for our bodies, but for our minds and spirits as well!

Trust the angel in you to guide your thoughts and prayers. Experience God's understanding and peace as you travel through your busy, stressful day.

And we thank God for our food. Amen.

How many times have we said table grace without giving a thought to the generosity of God's bounty?

Listen to the angel in you as she helps you feel truly grateful for your daily food and drink.

My Personalized Yummy List

- What is it about your favorite foods you like the most? The richness of chocolate? The juiciness of raspberries? The sizzle of a steak on the grill?

- Write your own, personal table grace expressing your thanks to God for providing you and your loved ones with such variety and plenty.

There's No Place Like Home

A warm and cozy home truly is a blessing. Take a moment every day to thank God for the four walls that shelter you from the wind and rain.

In your imagination, watch the angel in you sweep your stress and worry out the door. Say a little prayer to fill your home and heart with God's peace, warmth, and light.

Thank Heavens for FRiENDS and FAMiLy

Isn't it wonderful to have the support of special people when your road is rough and your burden heavy?

You may be tempted to isolate yourself in difficult times. Resist this temptation! Accept the caring gestures of others.

Give special thanks for the encouraging phone calls, the "thinking of you" notes, and the understanding smiles that are yours without even asking.

Your Supporting Cast

💗 Who are the people in your life who make you feel happy? Which friends and family members bring positive energy to your life?

💗 Write a thank-you message to share with the caring, giving angels in your life.

Share peace and understanding

Charity

Be an Angel of Mercy

One way to heal our own hurts is to help other people cope with theirs. The angel in you is ready and waiting to assist you in your caregiving!

Sometimes the people closest to us are the ones most in need of a lift. Visit a lonely neighbor. Donate an hour of baby-sitting to a stressed-out new mother. Take the time to listen carefully to the cares and concerns of the people you see every day.

Care for Mother Earth

Spending time outdoors taking care of our beautiful planet relieves stress and gives thanks to God, too.

You might volunteer to work with an environmental group or simply clean up a neighborhood park. You could plant a butterfly garden or nurse an injured bird's wing, walk the dog or feed the squirrels.

Staying in touch with all of God's creatures shows gratitude for the beauty of nature. And it helps you feel better, too!

♥ Draw a picture of yourself on the earth. What can you do right this moment to make it a better place?

♥ Draw a picture of your favorite flower.

The Power of One

Sometimes society's problems can add to your personal stress load. Listen to your angel. She knows that one person (you!) can help to change the world.

Become informed. Write a letter to the editor. Right a wrong. Take time to vote. Do what you can to protect the rights and safety of the poor, the weak, and the sick.

By expressing ourselves and working to make the world a better place, we can feel more empowered and assertive in our personal lives.

What would God want me to do?

Make a difference

Listen to your angel

Touch a heart

Share Your Special Gifts...

There's an old saying that goes, "Strangers are simply friends we haven't met yet." Helping "friends" in the community is another way to share God's love. When we give to others, we also care for our own needs. The Bible says, "Whatsoever you do to the least of these, that you do unto me."

Doing the right thing is great therapy. The angel in you is happiest when you're being an angel to others.

♥ **What are your skills? How could they help others?**

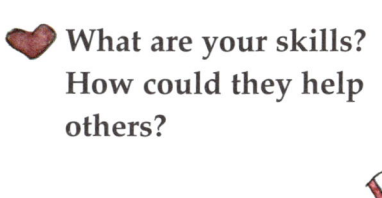

You Can Make a Difference!

♥ **Carve out a little spare time in the next month or so to call and offer your talents where they're needed.**

Keep in touch

Harmony

Old Buddies, Old Pals...

In our come-and-go world, some of our dearest friendships and support systems can change or disappear too quickly. Make an effort to find the people who've been important to you at different stages of your life.

Look up a childhood friend. Have lunch with a former co-worker. Track down an old roommate.

The history you've shared with these special people can remind you of the ups and downs you've already survived, giving you confidence to cope with today's trials.

Reach Out to a New Friend

Each human being has a unique, valuable perspective that can help you with your daily journey.

Of course, cultivating relationships takes time, energy, and effort. Ask the angel in you for the strength and courage to reach out and make a new friend.

♥ Who are some people you find interesting, positive, and fun?

♥ How could you approach these people about getting to know them better?

You can never have too many friends.

Friends From
9 ~ 90

Don't limit your friendships to people your own age. While it's true that people your age may share the same concerns and struggles, older and younger friends can offer fresh and valuable perspectives.

Older friends may have already survived the stress and problems you're facing right now. Their wisdom and insights can help you see beyond the present moment.

Younger people (even much younger people) can remind you to seize the day, to live this moment right now—and that life doesn't need to be so complicated.

Young or old, my friends are all angels.

Mend a Fence

Carrying grudges adds to your daily stress load. Pray for help in forgiving past hurts. Be tolerant of mistakes. Accept the imperfections and humanness of those around you.

Consider the people you've hurt, either recently or long ago. Apologize to those you've wronged—and while you're at it, forgive yourself, too.

♥ Think of a grudge or misunderstanding you'd like to heal.

♥ Write a script for contacting that person and making amends.

♥ Say a prayer for reconciliation.

Faith

Ride Out the Storm

Visualize a thunderstorm. Before it arrives, the clouds gather in the hot, muggy heavens. Discomfort and unease fill the air. Then lightning strikes, thunder crashes, and rain pounds. Life is tense and uncertain.

But when it's over, life is calm. You can feel the relief. The earth is nourished and cooled.

Think of your stress as an internal storm. Ride out your stress. Know that growth and peace can come tomorrow from the turmoil of today.

Growing Things

Have you ever thought about the simple act of planting a seed? What a leap of faith it is to assume this little thing will sprout and bear flowers or fruit to beautify and nourish the world!

Every day is full of opportunities for faith.

Believe in miracles.

Little Miracles

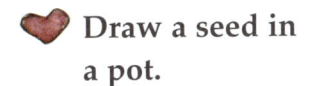

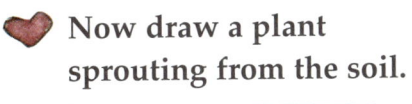

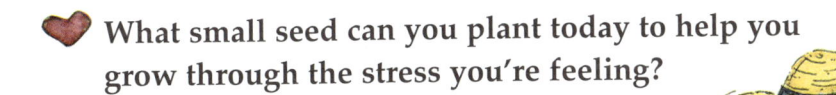

♥ Draw a seed in a pot.

♥ Now draw a plant sprouting from the soil.

♥ What do the seed and plant stand for in your life?

♥ What small seed can you plant today to help you grow through the stress you're feeling?

A New Day Dawning

Set your alarm to wake up before sunrise. The world is dark, and then, suddenly, magically, out of nowhere, a glimmer of light appears.

When our lives seem dark and hopeless, a similar light may be just beyond the next horizon. We must have faith, as the earth does each day, that the sunlight of hope and promise will return.

Starry, Starry Night

Standing under a twinkling midnight sky makes us feel insignificant and humble.

Contemplating the infinity of the universe can make our problems feel less overwhelming too. Listen to the angel in you: This too shall pass. God's good is greater than our stress!

Fly me to the moon!

💜 Pretend you're standing on the moon looking at the earth. What can you see?

💜 How big is your stress, in the grand scheme of things?

💜 Draw a picture of your stress, as seen from the moon.

Hope

Onward and Upward!

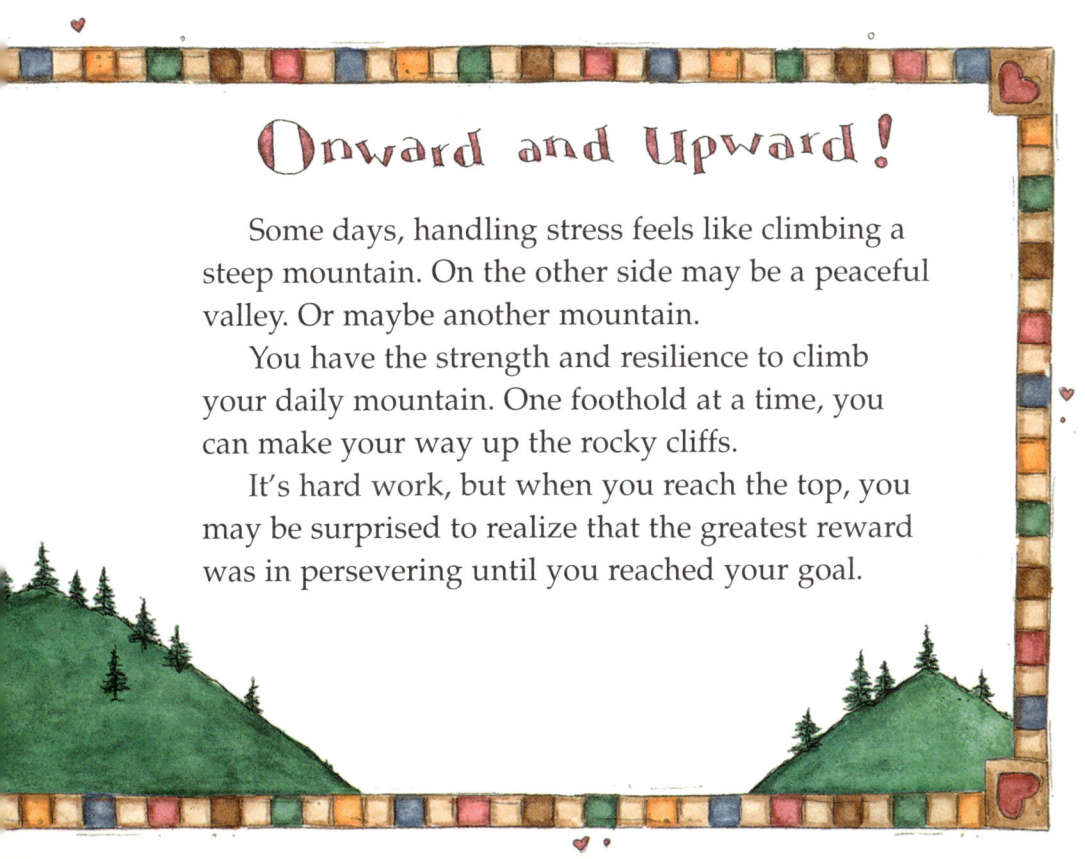

Some days, handling stress feels like climbing a steep mountain. On the other side may be a peaceful valley. Or maybe another mountain.

You have the strength and resilience to climb your daily mountain. One foothold at a time, you can make your way up the rocky cliffs.

It's hard work, but when you reach the top, you may be surprised to realize that the greatest reward was in persevering until you reached your goal.

To Everything There is a Season

Each of God's seasons has its own special meaning and beauty.

Spring is full of promise and growth. Summer nurtures us as we bask in its relaxation and warmth. Fall's brilliance and bounty precede a well-deserved rest. Winter's stark landscape brings solitude and serenity.

Each season of our life is beautiful in its own way. Our moods and experiences wax and wane, all part of God's magical rhythm.

♥ Draw a picture of the season in your heart.

♥ What have you gained from this season's experiences?

♥ What are you looking forward to?

The B·I·B·L·E

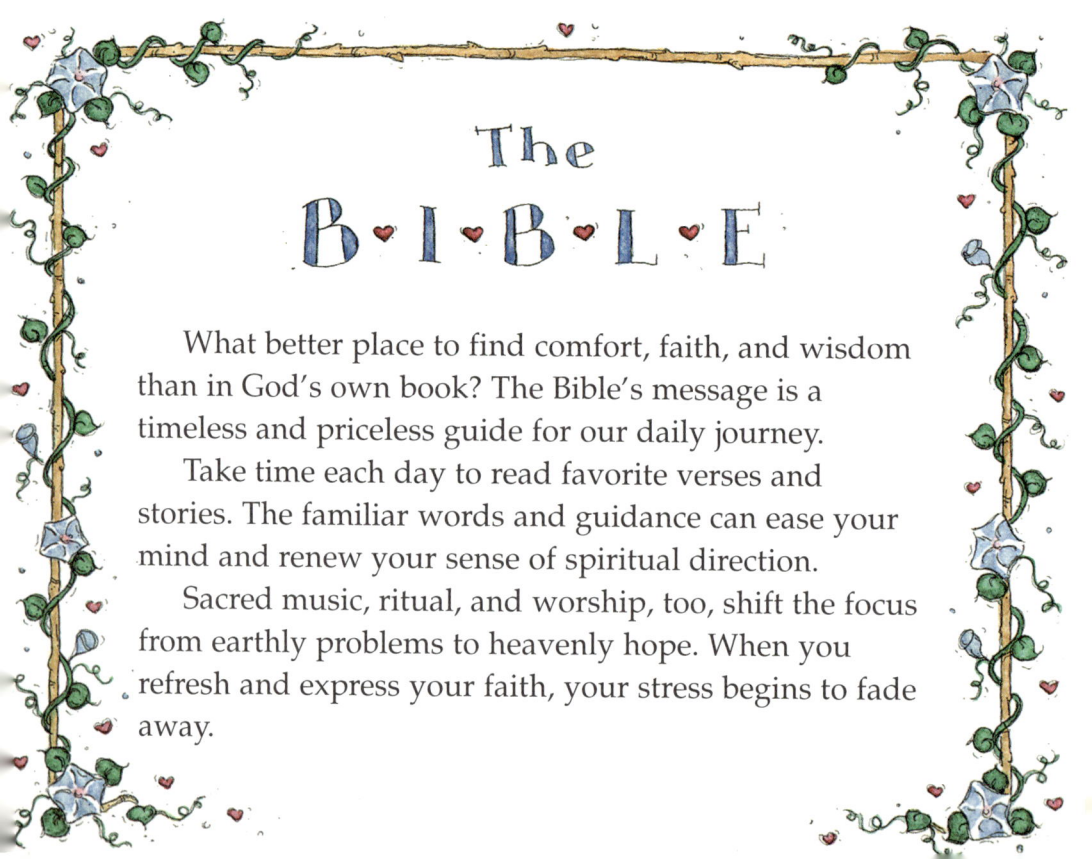

What better place to find comfort, faith, and wisdom than in God's own book? The Bible's message is a timeless and priceless guide for our daily journey.

Take time each day to read favorite verses and stories. The familiar words and guidance can ease your mind and renew your sense of spiritual direction.

Sacred music, ritual, and worship, too, shift the focus from earthly problems to heavenly hope. When you refresh and express your faith, your stress begins to fade away.

Take time each day

to refresh your faith

Treasure Wisdom

When you're feeling stress and anxiety, don't forget the wisdom of the ages. Philosophers, poets, and storytellers have been trying to make sense of the universe for thousands of years.

Visit your library or bookstore and find some thoughts to renew you and your inner angel.

❤ Find a quotation or story that comforts you in times of stress and worry. Keep a copy of it in a special place.

❤ What were the wisest, most valuable lessons you learned from your parents?

Help God Help You

The simple ideas in this book (or any book) may not always be enough to turn around an especially bad time. When life's burdens overwhelm you, seek the help of a friend, physician, clergyperson, or counselor.

God wants us all to be happy.

You're Not Alone
Believe
Hope
Harmony
Faith
God bless the Angel in You
Charity
Joy
Grace

Your inner angel is always there to help you. Even if you feel alone, or overwhelmed, or exhausted, your angel can give you strength to find the bright spots in a dark and troubled time.

Through the guidance of God, caring people, and your own inner angel, you can grow through stress and transform it into a positive force in your life. God bless the angel in you!

♥ **Draw a picture of your angel and you.**

About the Heavenly Ways Books

Once upon an idea, in a little heartland village, an artist named Deb Haas Abell toiled away with her paintbrush and paints. Inspired by the many angels in her own life, she created six heart-sprinkling characters: Faith, Hope, Charity, Joy, Harmony, and Grace. Their one mission in life was to spread the message that God gives each of us the ability to be an angel on earth...to touch lives, lighten hearts, and inspire souls.

These warmhearted spirits began to share their heavenly message through gift and greeting products in

Abbey Press's Angel in You collection. Before long, they were introduced to writer Molly Wigand, who translated their wisdom into books like this one—about Heavenly Ways to cope, even in the midst of life's hardships and heartaches.

But this is not just another pretty fairy tale. For Faith, Hope, Charity, Joy, Harmony, and Grace are present every day inside each one of us! May these books help you to discover your own inner angel...and may God bless the angel in you!

Heavenly Ways Books

Heavenly Ways to Handle Stress
Heavenly Ways to Heal From Grief and Loss
Heavenly Ways to Grow Closer as a Family
Heavenly Ways to Find Your Own Serenity

Available at your favorite bookstore or directly from:
One Caring Place, Abbey Press Publications,
St. Meinrad, IN 47577.
Phone orders: (800) 325-2511.

God bless the Angel in you